IMAGES
of America

DUNSTABLE

The profit of the field was not had without hard work. Members of the Tully family are shown here in the early 1900s stacking hay in a field on Fletcher Street. Hound Meadow Hill is in the background. In those times the profit was not always monetary, but was found in the support that existed between families and neighbors.

IMAGES
of America

DUNSTABLE
MAKING CONNECTIONS

Susan Tully and Susan Psaledakis

ARCADIA

Published by Arcadia Publishing,
an imprint of Tempus Publishing, Inc.
2 Cumberland Street
Charleston, SC 29401

Printed in Great Britain.

Library of Congress Catalog Card Number: 98-86388

For all general information contact Arcadia Publishing at:
Telephone 843-853-2070
Fax 843-853-0044
E-Mail arcadia@charleston.net

For customer service and orders:
Toll-Free 1-888-313-BOOK

Visit us on the internet at http://www.arcadiaimages.com

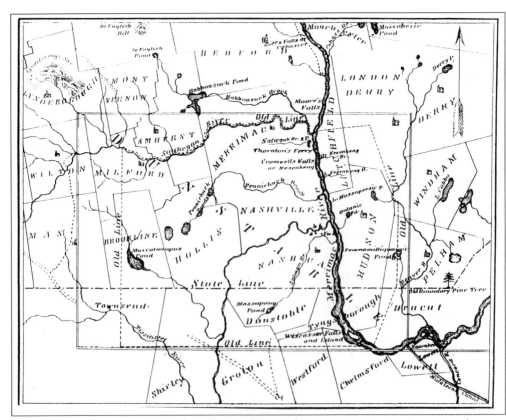

This map shows the original boundaries of Dunstable, encompassing 200 square miles.

CONTENTS

PREFACE

This project arose from our interest in the history of Dunstable and was fueled by the abundance of material we found available in the public library.

As the library prepares to move into its new home and the new century, it seems a particularly appropriate time to gather and share some of this information. Over the years, Dunstable has been the topic of newspaper articles, pamphlets, maps, books, and historical research by individuals and committees. The library has been the repository for much of this material. It is our hope to present it in such a way that both new and old families will have a better understanding of how Dunstable once looked and how it had evolved up to the early 1950s.

Often we found that our sources gave conflicting information about the date of a particular event or photograph, with inconsistencies varying from a year or two to as much as 50 years. Whenever possible we tried to verify the dates we used. If we were unable to do this we've shared the choices with you. There were also differing versions of events. We have been as accurate as we were able and invite comment, correction, or information.

Another challenge was how best to present the information. We decided to present the pictures of homes in geographical sections, much as you would view them driving through town. We limited the pictures of houses to those that date back at least to the early part of this century. The pictures of people and events in the final two chapters bring us into the 1950s.

We found it fascinating that there are still residents in town today who can trace their Dunstable connections back more than one hundred years, and some even to original settlers.

In talking with people about the history of their homes, many were not aware of their historical significance. Hopefully this book may provide a starting point for those who would like to learn more.

INTRODUCTION

Dunstable, incorporated on October 15, 1673, once comprised 200 square miles (12,800 acres) extending from Londonderry, New Hampshire, to Chelmsford, Massachusetts. It was originally incorporated upon the petition of 26 proprietors of land along the Merrimack. During the 1700s, section after section broke off until 15 separate towns were formed, leaving Dunstable only 10,500 acres and a population of 380 in 1790.

The original town was named in honor of Mrs. Edward Tyng, who emigrated from Dunstable in Bedfordshire, England. The Tyngs were among the early settlers of the land purchased from the Wamisit and Naticook Indians in 1661 for £20 sterling. As we travel through Dunstable today, we pass houses that can be traced back to some of Dunstable's original settlers . . . the Proctors, Cummings, Kendalls, Butterfields, Blodgetts, Swallows, and others.

Until 1732 Dunstable was the site of hardship and fighting because of the many struggles with local Native Americans. Every house was a watch house and every man a soldier. Wives and daughters were often left behind to man the garrisons. Later, the men of Dunstable were among the first to prepare for the American Revolution. Captain Leonard Butterfield led a group of Minutemen to fight in the Revolutionary conflicts of Concord and Lexington. Ebenezer Bancroft led a company of 50 Dunstable men at Bunker Hill. Volunteers again came forth in the 19th century, and Dunstable sent 64 soldiers to fight in the Civil War. Citizens continued to serve in the armed forces throughout our history and the names of many can be read on the Civil War, World War I, and World War II monuments in the town center. The chief concerns and values of the town centered around the family, the church, and the school. This way of life continued well into the 20th century.

Along the way the population climbed to 590 people in 1850 and then dropped to 408 in 1910. Some residents were perhaps lured away by the increased mobility provided by the automobile, and some left to find work in nearby mills. Tragically, an influenza epidemic claimed the lives of others who were living in Dunstable during this period. It was not until the 1950s that the town grew significantly and changes began to impact our way of life. This book covers the early history of Dunstable through the 1950s, showing how our town changed and grew up to that time in its history.

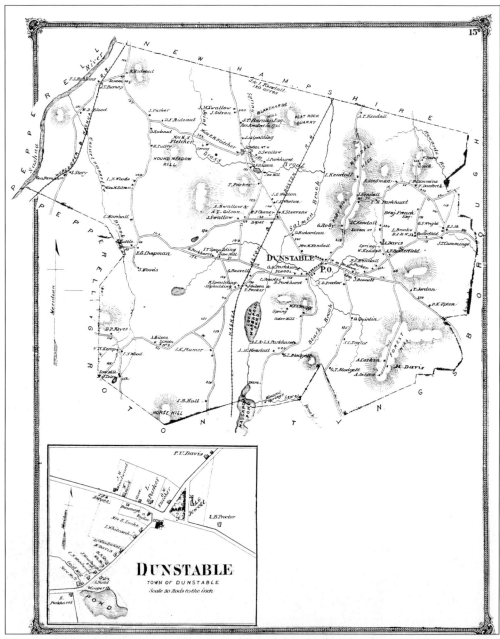

This map of the town as it was in 1875 was published shortly after the town's 200th anniversary.

One

THE NORTHEAST

Entering Dunstable from the east side on Route 113, we find the first indication of settlement in the presence of the Dunstable Town Pound. In 1768 it was written that "the pound in the west part stood and still stands beside the road from Dunstable Centre to Tyngsboro Centre, a little eastward of the homestead of Dexter Butterfield" (Nason 104). The 34-foot-square piece of land was sold to the town by Daniel Taylor for one shilling.

Immediately after the pound on the same side of the road is the current meeting place of the Tyngsborough-Dunstable Historical Society. This building is the Sarah Tyng Winslow School House. It was built in 1790 and served as a school until 1864. It was moved to this location and restored in 1968. The schoolhouse was a gift from Mr. and Mrs. William Farrow and the land a gift from Mrs. Margaret Larter.

#104 Main Street

This house was built for Capt. Josiah Cummings about 1795. His father, Oliver, served as a captain during the Revolution and Josiah, just a boy at that time, served as a guard. He later became a captain in the Dunstable militia. His grandfather, Nathaniel, was one of the first to settle in Dunstable. The road originally passed on the south side of the house; it was rerouted in the early 1800s. The house has been owned for most of the latter part of this century by the Cover family.

#155 Main Street

This house was built by Leonard Butterfield and his wife, Polly (Taylor), in 1783 on the site of an earlier structure owned by Robert Blood. It was near or on the site of one of the first garrisons. In the late 1800s it was the home of the couple's grandson, Dexter Butterfield. Elm Haven, as it is known now, is the home of Mrs. Margaret O. Larter.

#158 Main Street

Ida Butterfield James relates in her notes on Dunstable that when her uncle, Dexter Butterfield, inherited this property, it was a cider mill across from the main house (Gates 13). It was later used as a carriage house, which was turned into the home we see today. It is now the home of the Richard Olneys.

#194 Main Street

This house was built by John Nevin in 1731 on South Merrimack Road in Hollis, New Hampshire. It was settled in 1740 by Thomas Powers. In 1965, Judy and Edward Larter Jr. purchased the house and moved it to its current location. This is probably very close to the location of the first meetinghouse in Dunstable.

The Meeting House Hill Cemetery dates back to 1753, when the first meetinghouse was built near this site. The land was purchased from Lt. John Kendall and Ebenezer Butterfield. The first minister was Josiah Goodhue. The first meetinghouse was little more than a log cabin and had no pews or pulpit. In 1757 it was voted that each family should build its own pew, with those paying the largest taxes having first choice of location. The building was moved to the center of town on the site of the present town hall in 1791 and renovated. This sketch shows the meetinghouse as it looked after being moved and renovated.

#285 Main Street

This home was built by Asa and Pamela Butterfield in 1788. Asa's son, A.P. Butterfield, set up a trust fund to generate a scholarship for the highest-ranking Dunstable graduate each year. In 1997 this scholarship was awarded to Ben McGovern, who was also salutatorian of his class. In 1998, Nathan Edge, valedictorian, received the award. In the 1900s this was the house of John Kelley and later of the Vincent Best family.

A house was located on Route 113 between 285 and 383 Main Street and was probably built around 1777. It was built by Capt. Oliver Cummings and was long used as a tavern and on occasion as a meetinghouse. In the 1800s this was owned by Nathaniel Kendall, the son of Benjamin and Sybill Cummings Kendall. Only the cellar hole remains today.

#383 Main Street

Although some sources estimate that this house was built in 1870, it appears on the 1856 map as the home of a James Blodgett. The 1875 map marks it as the home of Libni Parker. In 1947 it was purchased by George McGovern and the land continues to be actively farmed by his sons today.

#416 Main Street

Built c. 1837 by Rev. Levi Brigham and his wife, Mary Fay, this house was later owned by Rev. Darwin Adams and, in 1875, by James Bennett. During the mid-1900s it was the LaViguere home; it is currently owned by the Bentley family.

#427 Main Street

Among the earliest houses, this Kendall homestead was built in 1730. Said to contain secret hiding places that were used when it came under Indian attack, it was granted a tavern license on February 8, 1743, and was known as the Ebenezer Kendall Tavern. On March 5, 1743, it served as the location for the first recorded town meeting held after the state line between Massachusetts and New Hampshire was drawn in 1741.

The Minutemen met here, and powder for their guns was stored in a barn across the road. This early view, looking westerly towards the house and barn with the cemetery beyond, might have been seen by a traveler entering town in the late 1800s. In 1856 the home was occupied by A. Jewett and in 1875 by Dr. Howe. It is now owned by the Hardman family.

Leaving the present center of town, we head north up High Street to the top of the first hill, known originally as Roby Hill. The farm depicted in these two pictures used to sit on the crest of the hill. It was the home of the Robys from the early 1800s. Gilman, Dexter, and Christopher Roby were born here. Their father, Samuel Roby, was a Minuteman in 1775.

Later this became the B.H. Brow home and the hill was referred to as Brow's Hill. The farm burned on June 25, 1925.

16

In 1908 Gilman Roby's second
wife, Sarah Read Spaulding
Roby, donated money for the
Roby Memorial Building, which
would serve as both library and
town hall for the rest of the 20th
century. Sarah was born in 1811
on the Read farm at the foot of
Blanchard Hill. She married
Abel Spaulding in 1836 and they
had one daughter, Sarah
Angeline. Her first husband, A.
Spaulding, died in 1843 and she
later married Gilman Roby.

Gilman Roby was the son of
Joseph and Betsy (Cummings).
He was born in 1808. His first
wife, Catherine, died at age 29
when she was struck by
lightening while brushing her
hair. Gilman had no children
with either wife. He was active in
town and continued to work the
farm throughout his life.

#166 High Street

This house was built in 1890 as an apple shed and then converted into one of many summer residences in Dunstable. The house was the home of Mr. and Mrs. Douglas and of Mrs. Douglas's daughter, Helen Sawyer. It is now the home of the Randy Hencke family.

Born in 1905, Dr. Helen Sawyer Hogg claimed residence in both Toronto and Dunstable for most of her life. She was a famous astronomer and author of *The Stars Belong to Everyone*. She was the first woman president of the Royal Canadian Institute of Astronomy. When in Dunstable she took pleasure in being involved in community activities.

#1 Thorndike Street

This house dates back at least to the mid-1800s and was one of the Kendall houses. It is now owned by the Burgess family.

#4 Thorndike Street

This is one of the original Kendall homes. It was built in 1756 by Temple and Abigail (Cumings) Kendall. Both the 1856 and the 1875 maps identify it as the home of their grandson, J. Kendall. This picture shows the farm as it looked in the 1950s before the barn burned and the outbuildings were destroyed. At that time the farm was owned by Palmer French, who sold one field after another until only the original house remained; that house is now owned by James and Betty Parker.

High Street at the top of Kendall Hill

The 1856 and 1875 maps show this as the Isaac and Mary Ann Kendall home, which stood at the top of the hill. In the early 1900s the Kennedy family purchased the farm and Donald Kennedy was born here. In the 1930s he removed the old house and built a new house behind the original site. Portions of the paneling and hearthstone from the old house were used in the new one.

#346 High Street

Built in 1896 by Faye Sargent, this house was alternately rented or unoccupied for the first half of the 1900s. The interior of the house remained unfinished and without plumbing or electricity until it was purchased in the 1950s by A.D. Kennedy. Currently it is the home of the Robert E. Kennedy family.

#473 High Street

This was the home of Deacon Zebedee Kendall and his wife and the birthplace of their son, Amos Kendall, on August 16, 1789. In the 1900s it became the home of Charles Glover. It is now the home of the Raymond Melancons.

Amos Kendall graduated from Dartmouth in 1811 with highest honors, later teaching school and studying law. He served as a tutor for the family of Henry Clay and was a chief justice of New Hampshire. Under President Jackson he held the position of fourth auditor of the treasury department and then of postmaster general.

#68 Thorndike Street

This home is thought to have been on this site as early as 1770. The location appears on the 1856 map as an E. Swallow home. For the latter part of the 1900s it has been owned by the Dumont family.

#85 Forest Street

Built by Captain Jonas Kendall in 1813, this house remained in the Kendall family until the 1950s. James and Lillian Kendall were the last of the Kendalls to live here. The house is now the home of Joan and Michael Nelson.

#99 Forest Street

This house was originally built abutting the Kendall House at 85 Forest Street. The two houses were connected by a common porch. This structure was separated and moved to its present location in the 1960s when the farm was purchased by Harold Blackey. The house is now the home of the Nowak family.

School House #1 was located just south of the Jonas C. Kendall house in the area of the current Nowak house. It was one of five schoolhouses that the town voted to build at a cost of $700 in 1805.

Originally this was the Moses and Susanna Davis homestead. The main house stood near the site of George McGovern's house (147 Forest Street), looking off toward the south with much the same view of the hills of Groton, Pepperell, and Westford that one sees from this point today. During the 1800s the farm stayed in the Davis family, passing from Moses and Susanna to their son, James Augustus.

A 1911 advertisement promoted the grandeur of this homestead: "'IDLEWILDE'—the most attractive Summer home in New England." At that time this was the estate of Arthur H. Hosford. It consisted of a main house, garage, blacksmith shop, stables, hen house, wagon sheds, carriage room, horse barn, corn house, and icehouse.

Mr. and Mrs. Arthur Hosford turned the Davis home into a social center in the 1890s. Here they are pictured dressed in their finery during one of the lavish balls that were often held at Idlewilde.

In its day, Idlewilde encouraged vacationers looking for rest, air and freedom to stay there. Among those who visited this lovely inn were Admiral Byrd and his wife and children. Here he is pictured on July 4, 1926, with his son, Richard Jr., after completing his memorable flight to the North Pole. Stories are told of his landing a small plane in one of the fields near the inn.

This picture shows the parlor of Idlewilde during the early part of this century. The house was sold at auction and purchased in 1911 by Bert Spaulding, who continued to run a successful inn there for years.

On May 13 in 1933, the reckless burning of this establishment was caused by the actions of a disgruntled chef. The destruction of this property was devastating to its owner and frequent guests.

Today only the garage remains on the opposite side of Forest Street from where the main house stood.

#167 Forest Street

On the 1856 map this property is identified as being owned by Leonard S. Butterfield (grandson of Leonard and Polly), and on the 1875 map by William and Catherine (Taylor) Kendall. It is now the home of the Rainis family.

#144 Thorndike Street

Built in the early 1800s, this home was once occupied by Lt. Paul Thorndike and his wife, Olive. Mr. Thorndike was a member of the first school committee in 1810. This location appears on both the 1856 and the 1875 maps as the home of an Ebenezer Stedman and his wife, Betsy (Blood). It is now owned by Rachel Roy.

#222 Thorndike Street

Thought to have been built around 1825, this was the house of Isaac P. Cummins in 1875. In 1997 it was left by Yolanda LaBlank to the Tyngsborough-Dunstable Historical Society.

#240 Thorndike Street

This house was listed as the residence of James T. Burnap in 1856. Burnap was active in town affairs, serving as town clerk in 1862, on the school committee in 1808, and as representative to the general court in 1870. He was the first superintendent of roads in 1871. By 1875 the house had become a Danforth home. It is now owned by the Starbird family.

#95 Hardy Street

Thought to have been built possibly as early as 1734, this location was the home of J.H. Kateley in 1856 and of a Cook family in 1875. In the early 1900s Ashley Hoffman lived there. In the late 1900s, David and Kendra Davidson added a pottery studio and shop. The property is currently owned by the Monk-Akerberg family.

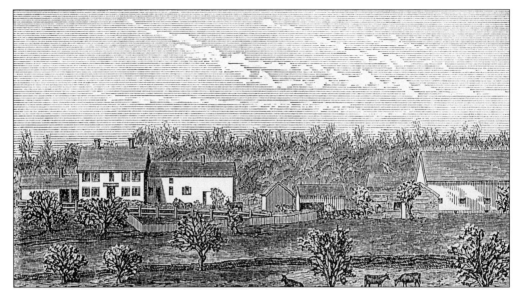

#94 French Street

This was the homestead of one of the earliest settlers of Dunstable, John French. Nason tells us that the earliest French lived in what later was used as a grain shed on this property. His name appears on the 1744 tax list, and his son John fought in the Battle of Bunker Hill. The current house was the home of his great-grandson, Benjamin French, whose granddaughter Adele married Leon Jeannotte and lived in the family home until the 1950s. This property is now owned by the McGoverns.

#20 French Street

This may have been the home of Thomas and Prudence Estabrooks, who appear on the 1744 tax list. It appears as Lawrence Brooks's home in 1856 and was also the location of a blacksmith and a wheelwright shop. In the later part of the 1900s it was owned by Marjorie Gustafson.

Two
THE CENTER

VIEW OF THE COMMON FROM TOWN HALL, DUNSTABLE, MASS.

This view of the center around 1911 shows the Dunstable Evangelical Church and the Union School.

#485 Main Street

This was the first of the Proctor family homes and was built by Ebenezer Proctor about 1733. It shows up on the 1856 map as the home of his grandson, Zephaniah P. Proctor. In the latter half of the 20th century, land was donated to the town by Zephaniah's descendent, Helen Proctor Mason, for conservation purposes.

In 1928 Warren and Idal Bacon purchased the house. They updated and remodeled the interior and lived there until 1962. It is currently owned by D. Tully.

#493 Main Street

The next house on Main Street has been referred to as "the newest of the Proctor Houses" or the Fourth Proctor House. The date of its construction varies from 1865 to 1873 to as late as 1896 in different sources. It was built by William Proctor, who served on the building committees for the Union School and the Roby Memorial Building. During the early 1900s it was owned by Thatcher Reed and is currently owned by Peter Georges.

#504 Main Street

This home was built by A. Nelson Hall around the turn of the 20th century. It was Nelson Hall who originally owned the land behind the church where members wished to build a horse shed. The story is told that he refused and the land was purchased by Calvin Austin and donated to the church. The house is now the home of the Crandall family.

#503 Main Street

Jasper Pope and Mary (Blood) Proctor built this home in the early 1800s. Jasper was the son of Jonathan and Rebeccah (Pope) Proctor. At some point between 1856 and 1875 this became the home of Ashur Jewett and later of his daughter Lizzie and her husband, Archie Swallow. They lived in this home until 1952 when it was purchased by C. Grasse. It was later owned by the Perras family.

Lizzie Jewett Swallow, born in 1864, was known to many as "Aunt Lizzie." She followed in her sister Clara's footsteps in serving as the town librarian from 1895 until her death in 1952. The library was initiated around 1878 and was located in Parkers Hall; it later moved to the cloakroom of the Dunstable Cornet Band Hall, and then to the west room of the Union School when that opened in 1895. In 1908 it found a home in the Roby Building. Lizzie's wish that the library would someday have a building of its own will be realized when the new library opens in fall of 1998.

Born on January 15, 1851, Archie Swallow was one of ten sons of Alpheus and Cynthia. In 1891 he married Lizzie Jewett. Like many of Dunstable's citizens at that time, he was not only a farmer but was also active in town government. He was a member of the board of selectmen, served as tax collector from 1895 to 1904, and as town clerk from 1911 until his death in 1937.

Florence Hampton served as assistant librarian under Lizzie Swallow and then took over as librarian in 1952, serving until 1983. She is also remembered as a town historian and was responsible for keeping scrapbooks of newspaper clippings and photographs in the library.

In 1790, Jonathan Proctor sold the parcel of land on which the town hall currently stands for 9£. In 1791, the first meetinghouse was moved to this site from Meeting House Hill. That building burned in October of 1864. From the time of that fire until the construction of the Roby Building, this land was the site of a bandstand and common, as no unified decision could be made on what to do with the property.

The Universalists formed their own society in 1818 and continued to use the meetinghouse after the Evangelical Society withdrew. In 1831 a new church was built on the corner of Main and Pleasant Streets by the members of the Evangelical Congregational Church. After the old meetinghouse burned in 1864, the Universalists tried to rebuild. The following poem describes the rift between the two societies. It was found among library papers.

Church Moving—1885

The Universalists on a September Day
Thought to build a chapel that would stay.
So the men and their teams, fourteen in number,
Carried onto the common all of their lumber.
They worked very hard from morn 'til night
And had the frame partly erected on the old church site.
But the Orthodox came the very next day
And took the precious thing away.

It was hard to see it torn down 'tis a fact,
And the public looked on in surprise at the act.
But 'twill be harder still I fear
For those who did the Common clear.
Ira B. Hall opened his gate
And offered to receive the whole estate,
But Zephaniah wishing to be a gallant host
Said he would take a part of the posts.

Dexter with a willing hand
Took a load of stone onto Jewett's land,
but he came out as mad as they
and told them to take their stolen stuff away.
They turned about in wild dismay
and carried them over across the way.
As they are no ornament to the street
we hope they will stay there 'til two Sundays meet.

Deacon Jones for the trench did go,
taking a shovel and a hoe.
He worked with right good will,
thinking the Lord would bless him still,
but he will find out 'ere he crosses the river
that the Lord can't bless the works of a sinner.
There were those there who helped the work to do
and they will all be ashamed before a year or two.

Nelson as we have often heard him say,
wished to have things go along in a legal way,
so Dexter and Daniel as white as a sheet,
took a walk down Main street.
And as they were gazing all around
the Chapel committee they soon found.
With shame and disgrace they looked on in wonder
and told them they might have all of their lumber.
But it stands there still behind the Church steeple,
with a cannon pointed to all the people.
They have disgraced themselves and their good old town
and I think that God in pity will on them look down.
But our conscience is clear and our Faith quite strong
that we shall have a church before very long.

—Anonymous

The first Dunstable church was actually erected in what is now Nashua, so that when the state line was drawn in 1741, the Massachusetts Dunstable Parish was in need of a meetinghouse. This was built in the area of the Meeting House Cemetery and then was moved to the present center in 1791.

Until the mid-1800s, the meetinghouse was the focal point of the community and was an integral part of daily life. The meetinghouse served as the gathering place where both town and church business were conducted. There was little separation of church and state, to the point that the first taxes of which we find record were used for the support of the teaching of the gospel. In his history, Nason tells us that the earliest selectmen were "invested with much more power than officers possess at the present day, and it was left with them to select a minister . . ."

In 1831, a congregational church was built slightly to the west of the present church on land purchased from Jasper Pope Proctor. By some accounts this building burned and was replaced by a new church in 1850. However, Mrs. Jonas C. Kendall presented a historical paper in 1904 stating that the 1831 church was enlarged and repaired in 1850 and more changes were made in 1888 when one of the chimneys fell. In her account there is no mention of a fire. We do know that the building burned on August 13, 1910.

It was decided that the new church should be very similar to the one that burned in 1910. It was built slightly to the east of the previous building. The building committee members were William P. Proctor, James E. Kendall, and Arthur N. Hall. The organ, which is still in use, was purchased with the help of funding from Andrew Carnegie. In 1947 the church reported a membership of 46.

This view of the Congregational church in 1850 shows the stained-glass windows which were one of its unique features.

#519 Main Street

Known as the Second Proctor House, this home was built by Jonathan Proctor in 1812 for his daughter Rebekkah when she married Josiah Cummings. In 1875 it was owned by George Washington Fletcher, and was purchased in 1908 by Calvin Austin. In the 1940s the Radinskys lived in this property and operated the Old Acres Inn. In the 1950s it was purchased by James Shaw, who served as town counsel. It is now owned by the Lamarre family.

The Austins called their Dunstable residence Calmore. This picture shows the sitting room during their ownership. The Austins were known as a very gracious couple, frequently opening their home for town events.

Rebekkah Proctor Cummings was born on December 14, 1794, to Jonathan and Rebeccah Pope Proctor. She married Josiah Cummings Jr. on August 27, 1812.

Josiah Cummings was born in 1783. When a post office was established on February 13, 1929, Josiah was named postmaster and held that position until 1852. He was also a representative to the general court.

Calvin and Julia Austin were summer residents of Dunstable and spent the winter months either traveling or at their winter home in Boston. Austin was the owner of the Eastern Steamship Line. During their time in Dunstable the Austins were active and generous members of the community. They lived at Calmore until 1945.

#40 High Street

Built in the early to mid-1800s, this was the Isaac Taylor home. Both Isaac and his son Isaac Jr. were deacons. Isaac was also the great-grandfather of Ida Rachel (Butterfield) James, whose story is told in *Dunstable Village*. The 1875 map shows this as the home of Deacon Thaddeus U. Davis. In the early 1900s it was part of the Austin Estate and was the home of Austin's caretaker, Sven Martinsen. In the mid-1900s it became the home of William Saunders and is currently owned by the Gallant family.

This picture shows how the center of town would have looked heading west on Main Street at the end of the 1800s and early 1900s.

#529 Main Street

Built by Edmund Page in the early 1800s, these buildings were originally used as a store and tavern. Page was a member of the Universalist Society and served as its clerk from 1818 until 1823. In 1854 the property was bought by Liberty Raymond and his wife, Sarah (Spaulding), for $1,500. By 1873 both buildings were owned by Libni Parker, who ran a store and post office in the second building. The house has been in the Wellington family for the past 50 years.

This hall, built slightly to the east of the main house, was at one time owned by the town. It was built by Jephtha Cummings in the mid-1800s and the selectmen held their meetings there. Space was set aside here for the first library, which was open from 7 to 8 p.m. on Saturdays and at noon on Sunday, with George Washington Fletcher serving as the first librarian. The Universalists met in the hall every other Sunday until the building burned in 1908.

#553 Main Street

This home was owned by Dr. Miles Spaulding in 1851 and then by Ira B. Hall in 1856. Hall was both a selectman and a constable. The 1875 map identifies the property as the J. Harvey Woodward house. In 1900 it became the Colburn house and is now owned by the Pare family.

#563 Main Street

This building was erected as a band hall for the Dunstable Cornet Band in 1860. It also served as a town hall until 1908. At that time it was purchased by B.H. Brow and used as a store and post office. After Brow moved his store, this became the home of his daughter, Frances (Brow) Day. It is now owned by her son, Howard (Pete) Day.

Byron Brow's first wife, Clara (Kruckman), moved with him from the Dakota territory to Dunstable in the late 1800s. They had nine children, three of whom continued to live in town. Their daughter, Frances (Day), and their sons, Howard and Elmer, have children and grandchildren here today.

#546 Main Street

In 1859 the church built this parsonage. At that time it cost $1,000 and its first occupant was the Reverend William C. Jackson. It was replaced in 1950 when a much smaller house was built next to it for this purpose. In the early 1990s the need for a larger home was met when a new parsonage was built on Brooke Street. The original parsonage is now the home of the Glinkas.

Marriage ceremonies were often performed in the parsonage. Pictured here are Lucy and Don Kennedy, who were married there on June 3, 1939. In 1934, at the age of 22, Alfred Donald Kennedy was the youngest selectman ever elected in Dunstable or in the state. He continued to be active in town politics throughout most of his life. His interest in and knowledge of the history of the town was often shared through a humorous story. Lucy (Duren) Kennedy was born in Carlisle. She continues to share her talent as an artist through her donations of paintings to the Dunstable Grange, and her love of music during "Music with Lucy" at the library.

#558 Main Street

Dating back to the 1750s, this house was the home of William Kendall. In the late 1800s, J.S. Jacques lived there. In the 1900s it was the home of Mrs. Amy James, who served as town clerk and collector of taxes. The house is now owned by K. Tully.

#576 Main Street

This house was built by the Page family, possibly in the 1860s. During the middle of the 20th century it belonged to Addison and Madeline Lowell. It is currently the home of the Kimptons.

#1 Pleasant Street

In the early 1800s, Edward and Anna Dunn, with their son William and his wife, Sally, operated a store here. William Dunn was the postmaster. The property was purchased in the 1860s by then Postmaster Oliver Taylor, and later by Postmaster George Butterfield. The post office continued to be located in this building. Butterfield served in this position from 1899 to 1913. In the early 1920s the building was purchased by the Goldthwaite family, who lived there throughout most of the 1900s.

This picture also shows the watering trough that was donated to the town by Jonas French. Jonas was a descendant of the original French family and lived on Hardy Street. His offer to donate the watering trough on the condition that the town would supply it with water was accepted at a town meeting on December 17, 1887. The trough furnished water for the weary traveler, whether man or beast. It was built with four different drinking heights: one for man, one for horse, one for oxen, and one for man's faithful companion dog.

#11 Pleasant Street

In 1856 this was the home of A. Parkhurst. By 1875 it was owned by Miss Locke; it later belonged to Alice Butterfield, the daughter of Georgiana and Dexter Butterfield. Ms. Butterfield owned the field behind the house and allowed it to be used freely by the town. She served as town treasurer and was the first woman to hold an elected office in Dunstable. The house is now the home of the Curtis and Sandy Gates.

#17 Pleasant Street

Both the 1856 and the 1870s maps indicate that this building was the home of a shoemaker, Lowell Whitcomb. In 1913 it was owned by a Harriet Hodgeman. The residence portion was known as Nutshell Cottage, and frequent references can be found to it in newspaper articles about town social events. In the 1920s Elmer Brow opened his store here and also housed the post office in a portion of the first floor. The building has continued to serve the town as a general store under several owners up to the present time. This picture was taken in the 1950s.

#22 Pleasant Street
Built around the beginning of the 20th century by Sara Roby, the house is pictured as it looked in 1923 during Dunstable's 250th anniversary celebration. Her daughter, Angie Parkhurst, is standing in front.

#29 Pleasant Street

This house appears on both the 1856 and the 1876 maps as the home of James C. Woodward, who served as town clerk from 1864 to 1866. He also operated a blacksmith and wheelwright shop. Through much of the 20th century it was the home of the Savilles and is now the home of their daughter, Frances (Saville) May.

Walter and Hattie May (Davis) Saville are pictured here with Sally Hogg. "Pop" Saville was an active member of the fire department.

#31 Pleasant Street

This was the home of Reuben Wright in 1858. In 1875 it was the home of Moses and Susan Davis, who moved here from the Davis home on Forest Street. They were the grandparents of Frances May. It is now owned by the Thompson family.

Looking down Pleasant Street towards the corner of Pond Street, at the time of this picture the house on the left would have belonged to the Wells family. The Hamptons' house can be seen on the corner. At an earlier time these would have been Woodward and Parkhurst homes.

#51 Pleasant Street

This house was the home of Charles Woodward in the mid- to late 1800s. The Woodwards ran a sawmill and a gristmill. The sawmill was located on the south side of Black Brook and the gristmill was on the north side. In the early 1900s the Loops lived here. It is currently the home of the Hoares.

#51 Pleasant Street

Originally the homes of brothers Charles and Jonathan Woodward were joined by an ell, but they were separated in the early 1900s. This house was moved to 73 Highland Street in 1992 and is owned by the Curley family.

#52 Pleasant Street

This home was built *c*. 1780 by Jonathan Woodward Jr., grandson of John and Hepzibar. The Woodwards ran a cooper's shop here. In 1856 the building was the home of Benajah Parkhurst; in 1873 it belonged to Mrs. Sabrina Parker Nudd, and for most of the 1900s it was owned by Miss Evelyn Wells and her parents. It is currently owned by the Amodei family.

This is a view of the center of town *c*. 1910, looking back from the corner of Pleasant Street and Pond Street. On the left side of the road are two Woodward homes. Next to those two structures is the barn of Moses Davis. On the right side of the street is the home of Evelyn Wells, with the new Union School in the background.

Three

THE SOUTHEAST
AND SOUTHWEST

This image looks westerly from the top of Forest Street. The home in the foreground belonged to Ebner Gilson in 1856 and then to Mial Davis in 1875. To the right is the home of Amos Carkin and to the left in the distance is that of Alvah Gilson.

#242 Lowell Road

Entering town on Lowell Road there were three houses dating back to the 1800s. The first would have been on the present Tyngsborough-Dunstable line and appears on the 1856 map as a Blodgett home. Continuing westward towards the center, the map depicts 242 Lowell Road as the Kimball Upton house. This later belonged to his son Peter K. and then to Norma (Upton) Puffer. It is currently owned by the Robinsons.

#164 Lowell Road

The third home pictured on the 1856 map was the Gilson home at that time. It is believed to have been built around 1800 by a Deacon James Taylor. He was born in 1767 to Oliver and Bridget Taylor. For much of the early 1900s, it was the home of Tom Baird. In 1955 the property was purchased by the Garvin family, who lives there today.

#160 Westford Street

This home was built in 1740 by Capt. John Cummings. It passed to his descendant, Ensign James, and his wife, Sarah (Wright) Cummings. It later was bequeathed to their son Allen and his wife, Maria (Blodgett). In 1875 it was the home of D. Quinlin. It is presently owned by the Biron family.

#408 Westford Street

The "old John Steele place," also known as Dunsbrikke, was built about 1740. John Steele was the first parish clerk of the area that was Dunstable in 1743. The house was built at the crest of one of the highest hills in town and was known for its panoramic view. The brick used in the construction of this house was fired in the yard from clay brought across the valley from the Parkhurst Farm on Pond Street. In 1856 it was the home of Samuel S. Taylor. During the later part of the 1900s it was the Farnsworth home. It is currently owned by the Flanagans.

#446 Westford Street

Currently the home of George Frost, this house was built by Josiah and Polly Spaulding in the 1790s. Records indicate that Spaulding leased this land from John Tyng. In the 1870s, the property was owned by George Thomas Blodgett. In the mid- to late 1900s, the Tom Mariner family lived here.

#165 Pond Street

Crossing the valley between Westford Street and Pond Street we come to the Cyrus Taylor house, built in 1856. It was later owned by William F. and Clara Chaney and then passed into the Goldthwaite family in the early 1900s. Willard Goldthwaite operated Twin Hill Farm, an active market garden, providing summer jobs for many of the young people in town.

#275 Pond Street

This land was purchased by Ebenezer Parkhurst in 1749. The present house is the second to stand on this site and was built between 1812 and 1830. The property remained in the Parkhurst family for about 150 years. The bricks were made on the premises, which also supplied the materials for the Flanagans' house on Westford Street. It was the home of Dr. Archibald, who had his office in the house, during the early fifties. It was later purchased by Arthur and Muriel Holmes, who raised four children there. Arthur Holmes has been active in community affairs, serving on the school board, board of selectmen, and the advisory board.

#328 Pond Street

This Blodgett homestead has been in the family for over two hundred years. Elden and Nathalie (Blodgett) Staples lived there for much of the 20th century and their son Paul and his wife, Joanne, now live there. The home was begun by William Blodgett in 1726 and consisted of what is now the living room. It was added to by his son Josiah in 1737. It was one of four garrison houses designated for the defense of Dunstable during the absence of Colonel Tyng. It is said that a Native American council rock is in the front lawn. This indicated that it was the place where the local tribes gathered for their council meetings and explains why there were frequent raids on the homestead built there.

#345 Pond Street

This Kendall homestead was probably built in the early 1800s either by Peter or by his father, Temple. This picture shows Peter Kendall and his son, Almond. Peter was active in town affairs, serving as selectman, school committee member, and representative to the general court. Both Peter and Almond were chicken and dairy farmers. In the early 1900s the Girl Scout camp was located on their property on Lake Massapoag. Kendall Grove, also owned by Almond, was a favorite picnic spot.

The first mill in this area was owned by a Samuel Adams. In 1688 he cut a channel through the natural dam at the "gulf" at Lake Massapoag. There he erected the first gristmill in Dunstable. The story is that one day, when called away, Samuel left the mill in the hands of a disgruntled servant. Water had been high and when a hole appeared in the dam, it went unchecked and the water broke through, sweeping away the dam, mill, and every other barrier. It flooded the valley below, creating a smaller pond now known as Lower Massapoag.

#70 Pleasant Street

Returning towards the center of town, on the corner of Pleasant and Pond Streets is the Hampton home. William and Florence Hampton lived there through the second half of the 1900s. They were both active in the community. The house was originally the Benajah and Laura (Swallow) Parkhurst home, built in 1823. The Parkhursts' daughter, Marietta, left $10,000 to the town to form a water district.

#87 Pleasant Street

This was originally the Americus Parkhurst house, built in 1823. Parkhurst was married to Sally Roby, sister of Gilman Roby. Their son, Owen, married Gilman's stepdaughter, Sarah Angeline. It was Sara ("Angie") Parkhurst who left money to establish the Parkhurst Free Lecture Fund, which continues to provide enjoyment to residents today. During the mid-1900s, the Downs family lived here. The house is currently the home of the Grahams.

This house was located near the site of Douglas and Janet Russell's home on Pleasant Street. It may have originally been a Spaulding home in 1875. At the turn of the century, it was the home of the Payne and Upton families.

#411 Pleasant Street

Now the home of Jane Lentz and Robert Frye, this house was occupied by Fred Fletcher and his sister, Florence Dow, for much of this century. Possibly built as early as 1756, the house was bequeathed by Ebenezer Parkhurst in his last will to Sarah Parkhurst (his wife) and Joel and Ebenezer Parkhurst (his sons). It later was the home of George Parkhurst. A nearby sawmill was run by the Parkhurst family until George Pierce purchased it in 1912 from Bertiz Parkhurst.

#460 Pleasant Street

This was originally the Curtin farm, built *c.* 1878 on land purchased from the Parkhursts. In the early 1900s it was bought by the Gosses and remains in that family today.

#690 Pleasant Street

This brick house is one of three in town, and was the home of Elbridge and Lucy (Parkhurst) Chapman. It was built *c.* 1800 by Elbridge's parents, Davis and Rhoda Chapman. The original house burned in 1910 and was rebuilt. It was the Shattuck home during the second half of the 1900s and is now the home of the Dalida family.

#701 Pleasant Street

The home of Anne and Robert Parkin was also a Parkhurst home. Thomas Henry Parkhurst's name appears on the 1856 map. He served on the board of selectmen in 1858. In the 1870s the home was owned by Charles Tuttle.

#64 Woods Court

Until the 1980s when this unpaved road was developed, the only house on the road was Samuel Woods's house, from which the lane eventually took its name. Woods was a stone cutter by trade. The house was passed on to his son, Summer. It has been lived in by the West family during the latter half of the 20th century.

#82 Kemp Street

On the 1856 map this appears as a Cumings property. John and Catherine Cumings were the parents of Dr. John Cumings, who became famous for his invention of the application of vulcanized rubber for dental purposes. In 1875 this was the home of Henry Toles. A sawmill was operated on the property by both residents. From the late 1930s until 1974 this was the home of William and Ada Simmons. It is now the home of Hugh and Roberta McGovern.

#219 Kemp Street

This was originally the home of Joel and Phebe (Cutter) Keyes, built *c.* 1812. It is currently owned by Harriet Hornblower.

Schoolhouse #2, built in 1846, was located about a half-mile from the center on Pleasant Street As in the other four schools that were built at this time, all grades were accommodated by this single room. It is now the site of the town garage.

This picture shows the Ira B. Hall farm, which was located on Hall Street near the Groton line. The home was destroyed by fire on October 12, 1932.

Four

THE NORTHWEST

The area northwest of the town center was less populated than the northeast side until the 1900s. Here we see section foreman Jim Stancombe checking the tracks. In the background is the home of Thomas Chaney, the stationmaster. This section of track was the longest straight piece of track in the B&M system.

#601 Main Street

This property was owned by the Blanchard brothers in the early 1700s. Records indicate that in 1778 a Dr. Ebeneser Starr lived there with his wife, Hannah (Blanchard). The property then passed to their son, Augustus. In 1856 it was the home of Asa Wood; in 1875 it belonged to Mrs. Kendall. During the early 1900s it was the home of the Berrys. The Murphy family purchased the house in 1952 and lived there until 1977. It is now the home of the Warren Church family.

This train depot stood at the intersection of Depot and Main Streets. It serviced the Nashua-Acton-Boston Line and opened in 1873 and continued until 1925. Chaney family members acted as stationmasters during this time. Thomas was the first and was followed by his son Charles and then by his granddaughter, Ethel Chaney Sargent.

#993 Main Street

Three different sources give three different dates for the construction of this house, ranging from 1730 to 1856. It seems likely that it may date back to the 1700s. It was the home of James Bennett in 1856 and of J.A. Spaulding in 1875. Owners in the 1900s included Arthur Bailey and, currently, the Urban family.

#1037 Main Street

Nason lists this house as among the oldest in town, built by Deacon Joseph Fletcher about 1735. Fletcher purchased 600 acres at 12¢ per acre in this part of town known as "Joint Grass." At the time of Nason's writing (1870s), the house was owned by James T. Burnap, Esq. Burnap was an active promoter of the Nashua-Acton-Boston Railroad, which opened in Dunstable in 1873. During the middle of the 1900s the house was owned by John Kenny. It is now the home of the Novak family.

#121 Depot Street

This house was built by Ens. John Swallow in 1757 burned in 1886 and was replaced by the current building, which is said to look much like the original. Swallow's descendents have continued to live there ever since. It is currently the home of Clifton Swallow Davis and his wife, Terry.

The grandson of John Swallow, Alpheus, served in the state legislature at one time. He established the first Dunstable Grange in 1874. He is also remembered as the father of the ten Swallow boys. Pictured here are Alpheus and his wife Cynthia with their sons. From left to right are (front row) George, Herbert, Cynthia, Alpheus, Harry, and Arthur; (back row) Archie, Willie, Myron, Sherman, Chester, and Marshall. Only three of the boys—Harry, Herbert, and Archie—remained in Dunstable.

#67 Mill Street

Possibly dating back to 1738, this house is identified as belonging to Jacob Parkhurst and his wife, Mary Ann (Reed), on the maps of both 1856 and 1875. It seems to have been in the Parkhurst family for nearly 200 years. In 1916 it was purchased by Mr. Swain. In the mid-1900s it became the Goubeaud home; it is now the Ferrari home.

#95 Mill Street

This home was built by Alpheus Swallow's brother, Daniel, in the mid-1800s. Daniel owned and operated a grist- and sawmill with his son Elfred until 1924 when the mill was destroyed by fire. Daniel also taught in one of the one-room schoolhouses in town. His granddaughter, Cora Swallow Reid, lived in the house until her death in the 1970s. Since that time her nephew, Archer Davis, has lived there with his wife, Bertha.

#3 Fletcher Street

This was the site of School House #4. The original building was converted into a summer home in the mid-1900s and later into a year-round residence.

#15 Fletcher Street

This house was built c.1820 and was the home of Miss E.R. Fletcher in the late 1800s. In the 1900s it was owned by the Whittiers and several other families. It is currently the home of the Drury family.

#34 Fletcher Street

This picture shows the original home of Francis Fletcher in the mid-1850s. It was later owned by Charles Menut until it burned in 1924. This is now the location of Paul Gay's home.

#291 Fletcher Street

Built *c.* 1856, this house belonged to David Rideout. Both David and his wife died within days of each other in 1918. The farm was purchased by Charles Tully and his wife, Bertha, and has remained an active farm in the Tully family since that time. It is currently the home of Charlie and Ruth Tully.

#401 Hollis Street

In 1793 this was the Silas Blood homestead. In the mid- to late 1800s it belonged to J. Parker. In the early 1900s this house was purchased by Charles and Bertha Tully, and is now the home of their son, George, and his wife, June (Lund) Tully Sr.

River Road School House #5

The children attending this schoolhouse were primarily from the Blood family.

#69 River Road

Now the home of the Timothy Munger family, this house was the home of Henry Blood Jr. and Rebekah (Read) Blood. They were married in 1826 and the house probably was built around that time. In 1856 it was the Wright home and in 1875 it was the home of Freeman Robbins.

#158 River Road

The original house was built *c.* 1793 by Eber Blood. The ell of this house was built in 1845 to enable the owners to take in boarders during the building of the railroad. In 1858 this was the home of Willard Robbins. When it was built on this spot, it was in the town of Groton. The town line changed back and forth several times until it was settled. In 1875 it was the home of Washington D. Blood. At one time this area was populated almost entirely by Blood families, and was known as Unkety Nassett. It is currently the home of Ann and Ronnie Patenaude.

#301 Hollis Street

This house was also a Blood house built in the late 1700s. It was the home of Noah and Mary (Chapman) Blood until 1856. Before the 1875 map was drawn, the property had passed to Henry Tully. His son Charles purchased the Parker farm and then the Rideout property that are currently farmed by the family. His daughter Clara lived here until her death in the 1950s. The home remains in the Tully family today.

#62 Hollis Street

Built c. 1839, this was the home of Clement and Betsy (Tolles) Marshall from 1856 until the late 1800s. It was later the Gardener Farm. During the 1950s it was owned by Edward Alan Larter. He constructed a modern barn and welcomed public visits to the dairy farm. In the late 1950s the barn was destroyed by fire. Today the house remains in the Larter family.

Five

WORK AND LEISURE

Life was simple and it didn't take much to keep children busy and happy. Shown here are Lottie Hannah and Ruth Tully (Choate) picking flowers at their Aunt Clara's.

This view features Massapoag Pond from Kendall's Point looking in a southerly direction. Pictured here are Van Staples and William Blodgett with Erwin Blodgett sitting on the ground on the Fourth of July in 1892.

This picture was taken near Blodgett's cottage looking north. In the canoe are Van Staples and his wife, Mary, accompanied by two guests.

The Union School was built in 1895 on land purchased from Ira Hall to replace the five one-room schools that had served the town up to that time. The Union School provided for the town's children without any additions for 75 years. In this picture fifth- and sixth-graders gather in front of the Union School at the request of a photographer taking pictures for postcards of Dunstable in the fifties.

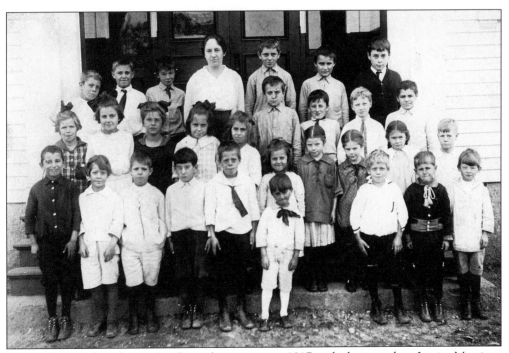

First- and second-graders gather for a class picture in 1917 with their teacher, Louise Morrison Brow. She later served as postmaster.

Dunstable's baseball team is pictured in 1887. From left to right are William Proctor, Arthur Butterfield, A. Nelson Hall, Leroy Woodward, Paul Myette, James Kendall, George Searles, James Tolles, Frank Sargent, Henry Tolles, Elmer Chaney, Jamie Woodward, Henry Parkhurst, and Harry Tolles.

Union School students appear here in 1926. Grades five through eight were taught by Mr. Lincoln. Some of the students pictured here are as follows, from the left: (front row) third is Stuart Chaney and fifth is Alfred Dixon; (middle row) fifth is Bea Drew, eighth is Mildred Tully, and twelfth is Ruth Townsend; (back row) first is Bobby Menut, second is Howard Drew, fourth is Frances Saville, fifth is Ruth Loop, seventh is Jane Dugan, eighth is Hazel Smith, ninth is Ethel Tully, tenth is Danny Chartier, and eleventh is Ray Chartier.

One of the earliest school buses was pulled by this team of horses. Before the Union School opened in 1905, children would walk to their district school. In inclement weather it was up to families to provide transportation.

Grades one and two appear here in 1934. They are, from left to right, as follows: (front row) second is Joe Craven, fifth is Lawrence Goldthwaite, seventh is Mary Davis, and eighth is Virginia Goldthwaite; (middle row) third is Freda Bashler, fourth is Herbert Sargent, fifth is Peter Day, sixth is Johnny Goldthwaite, and eighth is Francis Conndly; (back row) Arthur Jennette, Vernon Bodwell, Henry Goldthwaite, and Ervin Drew.

Here we see one of the first motorized school buses.

In the winter the wagons were put away and the team was hitched to "barges" or "pungs." Clara Tully—shown here with her horses, Jesse and Gentry—was one of the drivers.

A horse-drawn tank wagon travels along Pleasant Street.

This was an early dump wagon drawn up in front of a house that had recently burned. This type of wagon was used for hauling materials.

Notice the right-hand drive on the 1915 Model T touring automobile. The driver is Alfred Dixon, the Austins' chauffeur, with Ida, Andrew, and Moses Stancombe.

Harry Swallow is the driver of this vehicle crossing the tracks on Depot Street. Clara and her father, Herbert Swallow, are in the back seat.

Frank Sargent with his son, Conrad, stopped to chat with Clara Swallow.

Clara Tully was known for the ease with which she handled animals, large and small. Here she is with one of her horses.

Sargent's icehouse was located on Woodward's Pond. Ice-making was a major business during the late 1800s and continued even until the 1940s. During the winter months the ice, often as thick as 16 inches, was harvested and packed away to be used during the summer months.

The C.H. Burke Baking Co. would deliver breads, cakes, and pies to your door.

Another common business in town was the milling of lumber. Some sawmills were portable and could be set up where needed and then moved on to another location. This one was on Hollis Street at the time of this picture.

In the late 1800s and early 1900s a good team of horses was a necessity on a farm. Here we see George Tully driving his team with a load of logs.

Brothers Harry and Herbert Swallow delivered milk to Lowell in the early part of this century.

This picture shows the highway department c. 1918 picking up a second hitch before beginning the work of grading the road. The man at the rear of the wagon worked a wheel that would raise or lower the grader that was under the wagon. Although motorized vehicles were available, much work was still done with horses. When this picture was taken, Frank Sargent was the highway superintendent and may be one of the men pictured on the wagon. Charles Tully and his brother George are standing beside the wagon.

Here we see Charles Tully raking hay into windrows that would later be stacked and stored away for the winter.

Mr. Moss, the blacksmith, would travel from town to town, calling at farms and keeping the horses fit.

Here we see Charles's sister, Clara, with one of her cows. Waneta, a ward of the state, is seated at the milking end of the cow. With only a few cows, milking could easily be done in the open.

Howard McLoon, Arthur Ford, and Walter Saville are seen in 1954 as they load up a truck with hay from the baseball field behind the store. Haying was hard work whether it was done with horses, trucks, or tractors.

Grace Lull and a friend on her left are pictured here finishing off a load of hay. If loose hay is not loaded properly, the hay and anyone on it ends up back on the ground. Both men and women were needed in the hay field.

Helen Jones (Kennedy) helps out with haying at Clara Tully's.

A major crop on the Tully farm was potatoes. Here Eugene Tully, Donald Hannah, George Tully Sr., Henry Hannah, Charles Tully Sr., and Hamilton Dolby show their harvest in 1940.

During the winter months, it was time for logging. George Tully Sr. stands beside a load of logs headed for the mill.

Johnny Goldthwaite is pictured here in 1941 with a load of fresh vegetables ready to go to market in Boston and Charlestown.

It was a beautiful sight to see the field next to the church full of squash when driving through the center of town. Here, a load of Willard Goldthwaite's blue hubbard squash heads to market on the back of Charlie Adamowich's truck.

The Hurricane of '38 took its toll in Dunstable, as it did elsewhere. Here we see the cutting up of a large oak tree that came down during the storm on the Swallow farm. From left to right are Howard Drew, Harry Swallow, Alfred Drew, Herbert Swallow, and Richard Drew (to the right of the logs).

Six
MEMORABLE OCCASIONS

The town voted to expend $500 for a bicentennial celebration in 1873. Another $120 was privately donated and plans for the event began. A committee was chosen and included members Josiah Proctor, Dexter Butterfield, James Swallow, Jonas Spaulding, John Parkhurst, William Kemp, Washington Blood, Ira Hall, George W. Fletcher, and Chairman Benjamin French.

September 17 was chosen as the celebration date. On that day a parade assembled and proceeded from the railroad depot to the center. A speaker's stand was erected on the common. A banquet was held and music enlivened the festivities. Over 3,000 people attended this event.

Cora Swallow, granddaughter of Daniel Swallow, was born *c.* 1885. After attending the Union School and then high school in Nashua, she attended the Fitchburg Normal School. She taught school in Newton for 18 years and then returned home to care for her ailing father. She married Herman Decature and several years after his death married Clarence Reid.

She was the first woman to be allowed to assist in the town meetings and elections. She was an active member of the grange and took an avid interest in the library, often helping her Aunt Lizzie. This picture was taken in 1903, at the time of her high school graduation

Laura Davis was the second wife of Deacon Thaddeus Davis. Later in her life she lived with her daughter, Marita, wife of A. Nelson Hall. When she died in 1919 at the age of 104, Laura was considered one of the oldest people in the United States.

This picture was taken on August 14, 1910, the morning after the Evangelical Congregational Church burned.

This millstone can be seen today in the Central Cemetery. It was brought here from the Swallow gristmill on Mill Street.

99

A victory parade in 1918 celebrated the end of WW I. The children are marching down High Street.

Ernie Sweet is pictured here next to his father's ice truck. The Sweets moved to town in 1930 and bought a large tract of land from James Kendall. Salmon Brook flowed through their land, providing water for a man-made pond. They began an ice business that continued to operate until 1949. They also ran a store and garage on Pleasant Street

Dutch McWilliams and Bud Savage are at Camp Massapoag in 1921. They were ready for camp, but was camp ready for them?

This picture shows the preparation of a baseball field at the camp in 1924.

Ready! Get set! Go! The YMCA at Lake Massapoag has provided summer fun since 1919.

This picture was taken at the camp in 1924. These giant slides were a favorite among campers.

Calvin Austin and Alfred Dixon are shown here as they pause on their horses during an annual fox hunt.

The fox hunt took place each fall with members of the Groton Hunt Club arriving at the Austins' early in the morning.

Levi Lawrence was a staunch supporter of the Congregational church. After the 1910 fire, he donated $1,000 to restore the basement for use as dining hall, kitchen, and meeting room while the rebuilding was in progress. When he died in 1914 at age 85, he left a legacy of $2,000 to the church.

Laura (Parkhurst) Lawrence was born in 1826. She was the daughter of Benajah and Laura Parkhurst.

The Swallows have been holding family reunions for more than one hundred years. This picture was taken in 1920, when the Swallows had been in town for nearly two hundred years.

Born in Dunstable on the Swallow Homestead on Depot Street on December 3, 1842, Ellen Swallow was the daughter of Peter and Fanny. She was the first woman to receive a degree from MIT and went on to become a member of the faculty there. She was an activist for women's rights. She began the science of ecology and founded the American Home Economics association in 1908. She married Robert Richards, also an MIT faculty member. The addition to the Union School is named for Ellen Swallow and in the early 1990s the town recognized her contributions by designating December third as Ellen Swallow Day. This was accomplished through the work of Ms. Anne Polaski's fifth-graders at the school.

In the early 1900s, family pictures were few and far between and posing for them was usually considered a special event. Charles and Bertha Tully are shown here with 6 of their 11 children. From left to right are Henry, Charles Jr., Bertha, Ted, Myra, and baby Ethel (held by her mother).

This is a picture of a Parkhurst family reunion in the late 1800s. At the time of this picture the home on Pond Street was owned by Parkhurst brothers Albert and John.

The Dunstable Cornet Band was organized on September 15, 1861, with Hiram Spaulding as leader and manager. The band members were small in number, averaging about 18. Although they called themselves the Dunstable Cornet Band, they were in fact a brass band that included cornets, tubas, and one trombone. The trombonist was Ellis Brooks, who later played with John Phillip Sousa and the United States Marine Band.

The band was unique in that members played their instruments while mounted on horseback. They were outfitted in the grandest fashion, in long navy blue coats trimmed in a profusion of gilt braid and with gold epaulets on the shoulders. They wore visor caps trimmed with a red-and-white fountain plume.

During the band's almost 40 years of existence, they played not only locally but were featured throughout the state at fairs, celebrations, and at military funerals. The group disbanded in 1897.

The town hall and church were draped in red, white, and blue as the town prepared to celebrate its 250th anniversary in 1923. In this picture preparations are being made for the events later in the day. The anniversary picture of all the townspeople was taken here.

The church joined in the celebrations. The minister at that time was Rev. Alvin P. Cummins. Rev. Henry A. Parkhurst was one of the guest speakers and "president of the day." (*Lowell Courier*, September 6, 1923.)

Several tents were erected in Alice Butterfield's field and luncheon was served under the direction of John Whittier and his committee. The lunch was provided by D.L. Page and Co.

At that time John Kelley, Harold Goldthwaite, and Harry Swallow were the selectmen. Col. Arthur Butterfield presided as toastmaster. He was one of the original Butterfields that had been reared for 15 generations in the Dexter Butterfield homestead.

Sarah Angeline (Spaulding) Parkhurst was the daughter of Sara Read Spaulding and Abel Parker Spaulding. She married Owen Parkhurst and lived in what is now the Grahams' house. Later in life she moved in with her mother (Sara R.S. Roby) in the house next to the fire station. Like her mother she was generous to the town, leaving money for the Parkhurst Lecture Fund.

Nat Kendall, son of William and Catherine (Taylor), was born on Kendall Hill in 1853. In his youth he was a blacksmith's helper. He later moved to Malden where he worked in a shoe shop. He returned to Dunstable when he married Emma Chaney. He was the janitor at the Union School and at the church for many years. He was also an original member of the Dunstable Cornet Band and lived to be one of the oldest remaining members in Dunstable. Here he is pictured in his band uniform.

This picture of Brow's Store was taken in the early fifties. This was the store's second and newer set of gasoline pumps. The post office was still located in the store at this time. You can see that the price of gas was 29¢ per gallon.

Howard Brow was one of Byron and Clara's nine children. He was born in 1900 on the Brow farm on High Street and lived in Dunstable for some years after his marriage in 1935 to Margaret Davis. They eventually moved with their family to Chelmsford. His brother, Elmer, and sister Frances ran the store and post office in town for many years. His son, David, now resides with his family in town.

Although pictured in front of the "new" fire station, this was the first ladder truck purchased by the town. Before the station was built in the fifties, fire-fighting equipment was stored in the horse sheds and then in Walter Saville's garage.

This picture shows a newer fire engine parked next to "Pop" Saville's garage. His grandchildren, Iona and Arthur Ford, are on the truck.

Herbert Swallow, who was one of ten boys, had just one daughter. She was Clara J. Swallow. She married Clayton Davis and had eight children. She was very active in the community, perhaps best remembered as the moving force behind the minstrel shows that were presented during the forties and fifties. Not only did she raise her own eight children, but she cared for many other children in town.

This was one of the many minstrel shows directed by Clara Davis. Participants in this "North American Chorus" were as follows: Victor Blanchard, Charles and Eleanor Blumenauer, Frieda Carter, Ann and Daniel Chartier, Minnie and Walter Fry, Lillian Hampton, Betty Kenny, Patsy Kenny, Dorotheia Chartier, Louis Chartier, Mary Cover, Monica Ferrette, Frances Ford, Rosalie Lynch, Rod McDonald, Barbara and Irving Meridith, Melita Patch, and John Yale.

"The Jolly Selectmen" featured Arlene Delisle, Martha Davis, and Gloria Dunn. During the war years the town was assigned the amount of $11,000 as its quota to be raised for the purchase of war bonds. They exceeded this by raising $17,000, much of it through the sale of tickets to the minstrel shows.

"Fle-Hill Duet" featured Andy Ferretti and Frank Frisselle. This duo, along with other acts, was so popular that they were invited to perform in surrounding towns.

114

The traditional minstrel shows continued to be popular for many years after the war had ended. "Bell-Bottom Blues," another act from an early '50s show, included Loretta Upton, Barbara Yale, and Carol Brown.

Always popular, these versatile performers included, from left to right, (front row) Forest Bourbonnie, Charles Blumenauer, Pete Scuito, and Clifton Davis; (back row) Ann Chartier, Martin Durkin, and Betty Kenny, and Cora Goldthwaite.

Hundreds of troops from Fort Devens used the Hollis Street area for practice maneuvers during WW II.

The troops were taught survival, often camping in the woods and living off the land. It was reported, however, that you might awaken in the morning with a soldier who had slept under your window begging for something to eat.

Here a military jeep rolls along an unpaved road.

Military transport trucks were a common sight during the war years.

Dunstable's veterans gather around the WW II memorial in front of the town hall. Pictured here are, from left to right, (front row) Elmer Brow, Addison Lowell, Helen Bailey, Eleanor Goldthwaite, Geraldine (Corn) Dumont, Leo Dumont, Gerald Dumont, Cliff LaPorte, Arthur Gosselin, and Ed Colburn, Sr.; (back row) Claude (Sonny) Day, Sonny Colburn, Marcel LaViguer, Gordon Brow, Bill Brow, Charles Staples, Jack Debarbian, Maurice (Buzz) Drew, and Charles Blumenauer.

Bill, Doris, and Gordon Brow, the children of Louise and Elmer Brow, were all in the service during WW II.

Willard was a 4-H leader for many years. Here he is pictured with, from left to right, (front row) Richard Marley, Linda Brown, Jackie Brown, David Hardman, David Marley, and Eugene Chaney; (back row) Richard Headlund, Carol Brown, Willard Goldthwaite, Joseph Marley, and Teddy Hardman.

Willard Goldthwaite and Arthur "Brother" Ford take a brief rest while working in the garden.

The Dunstable Grange Fair has been the major event in town at the end of every summer for the past 70 years. Here is Flora Upton holding Brian and Edna Stevens watching over her son, Richard, in 1946.

One of the old-time favorite events of the fair was the Tiny Tots Parade, which featured children under six years old in costumes with their favorite decorated wagons or tricycles. Here we see Gerald Simmons on his tricycle and Mary Ann Goubeaud with her doll carriage at the front of the parade.

Sally Craven may have been the winner of this parade!

For the older children there was the Horrible Parade. The costumed Indian in the middle later served two terms as the town's first woman selectman. Standing with her back to the photographer is Mrs. Shaw, who organized the parade and other events for children.

The fair presented an opportunity to show the best of the summer crops. Here we see Ida Wellington, Frances Ford (May), and Ben Wellington placing ribbons on the winners. In 1998 the grange celebrated the 72nd anniversary of the fair.

"At a Grange Fair, this lovely group of ladies was deemed Best Farm Crop" (*Lowell Sun*, 1950). Walking down Common Street from left to right are Harriet Morgan, Helen James, Viola Bodwell, Evelyn Dow, Barbie Goldthwaite, Louise Goldthwaite, Ann Davis, Doris Brow, and Barbara Colburn.

The Women's Degree Team was in charge of the grange initiation. Here pictured from left to right are as follows: (front row) Bernice Dumont, Sally Davis, Marion Pillsbury, Ann Davis, and Edna Hersey; (second row) Cynthia Goldthwaite, Marjorie Field, Gertrude Green, and Lorraine Dumont; (third row) Barbara Colburn, Helen James, Ruth Brow, and Mildred Tully; (back row) Mrs. Upton, Amy James, Barbara Goldthwaite, Helen Bailey, and Mabel Goss.

Attending a grange installation from left to right are Gladys Craven, Frieda Carter, Frank Carter, and Ann Davis Chartier.

Scouting was an important activity for Dunstable's young people. Pictured here in the front row are Barbara Colburn, Dorothy Goldthwaite, Rosalie Goldthwaite, Helen James, Corrine Bacon, Virginia Stancombe, and Lucille Morgan. This picture was taken in the 1940s.

Girl Scout leader Frances Ford (May) and her daughter Iona are pictured here in full scout uniforms. Mrs. May was a scout leader for many years and has held scout membership for 60 years.

Girl Scouts working on a Wild Flower Badge purchased a blue spruce tree in 1957 and donated it to the church. Here, planting the tree, are Jean McGovern, Susan Kennedy, Charlene Weisberg, Elizabeth Holmes, Gladys Craven, and Donna Bourbonnie.

The church also provided activities for youth. In 1886 a Society of Christian Endeavor was organized and continued to be popular with young people well into the 1900s. It was followed by the P.F. (Pilgrim Fellowship), which was an important part of growing up in town in the fifties. Some of the youth pictured here include Dickie Stevens, Howie Rich, Billy Murray, Alan Chaney, Robert Kennedy, Jackie Brown, Iona Ford, Dottie Bowen, Linda Brown, Mary Ellen Lehtinen, Sally Craven, Reverend Clyde, and Bonnie Reid.

Celebrating the Fourth of July in front of the Kennedys' summer camp on the farm from left to right are as follows: (front row) Margaret Brow, Betty Savage, Waldo Savage (minister from 1937 to 1940), Ruth (Kennedy) Chaney, and Stuart Chaney; (back row) Lucy Kennedy and Howard Brow.

The 65th anniversary of John and Grace (Clark) Upton was celebrated on October 24, 1953. Many friends and relatives joined in the festivities. Although they had no children of their own, the Uptons raised six boys on their farm. Loretta and Brian Upton are pictured here with them.

Charles Glover celebrates his 90th birthday with friends and family on March 23, 1958. He served as constable and police chief and as the church Sunday school superintendent for many years. Here he is shown seated on the right with his cousin, receiving congratulations from then-selectman George Tully Sr. and Archer Davis.

In 1947 Governor Bradford visited Dunstable and gathered with residents on the town hall steps for picture taking. From left to right are as follows: (front row) Selectman James Kendall, the governor, Ray Chartier, and Selectman Ed Colburn; (second row) William Hampton, Ted Patenaude, Town Counsel Martin Durkin, Ray Chartier, Florence Hampton, unknown, and unknown; (third row) Johnny Goldthwaite, Selectman George Tully Sr., Jack Debarbian, Mr. and Mrs. Douglas, and two unknown persons; (back row) Charles Grasse and, at the end of that row, Mrs. Whittier and Lillian Kendall.

The first Little League teams were formed in 1953. Danny Chartier was the coach for the Indians and Charlie Blumenauer was the coach for the Red Sox. Pictured here are the Indians. From left to right are as follows: (front row) Robert Kennedy, Kenny Robbins, John Goubeaud, Tommy LaVigueur, Howard Rich, Dickie Chartier, and Gary Drew; (back row) Joe Lynch Jr., Teddy Hardman, David Marley, Dickie Kenny, Jeff Best, and James Dow (Sr.).

Sources

Gates, Curtis. *Dunstable Village*. Nashua, NH: Accurate Printing, 1973.

Nason, Elias. *A History of the Town of Dunstable, Massachusetts*. Boston: Alfred Mudge & Son, 1877.

Vital Records of Dunstable Massachusetts to the End of the Year 1849. Salem, MA: The Essex Institute, 1913.

Acknowledgments

We wish to thank the following groups and individuals for the loan of pictures and for their generous sharing of information and memories:

Dunstable Public Library, Tyngsborough-Dunstable Historical Society, Dunstable Historical Commission, Selectmen's Secretary Danice Palumbo, Assessor's Secretary Maria Hars, Jennifer Kimpton of the YMCA Camp Massapoag Family Outdoor Center, George and June Tully, Lucy Kennedy, Ann Butterfield, David Brow, Alan Chaney, Frances May, Ernie Sweet, Paul Staples, Laura Tully, Willard Goldthwaite Jr., Robert Frye, Jim and Shirley Hoare, Peggy Perras, and Tom and Erin Costello, and the staff at the *Lowell Sun*. All royalties and proceeds from private sales of this book will benefit the Dunstable Public Library.